LAUGH OUT LOUD CANADIAN NATURE

SAHARA KAGUME

iThink Books

Contents

Canadian Creatures

Canada is a vast land that has many fascinating and unique creatures.

Some, like the mighty muskox, live in the coldest climate in the world.

Others, like the American Pika steal from their neighbours.

Still others, like the spotted skunk, are little furry acrobats.

Read on to learn more about the lives of some of our wild Canadian neighbours.

Bald Eagle

Bald eagles often steal prey from other birds rather than catch their own.

What's an eagle's favourite dog breed?

A Beagle!

They will sometimes play together in the air by throwing sticks back and forth.

Bald eagles don't get their white head until they are about 5 years old!

Bald eagles live year round along the coast of British Columbia. During the breeding season, they can be found throughout much of Canada, in forested areas near a water source.

In Indigenous culture eagles are seen as medicine birds and are treated with great respect. They are also seen as a connection between humans and the Creator.

Steller sea lions are pinnipeds, which means that they have flippers on the front and back of their bodies.

The males are much bigger than the females.

Females usually live 10 years longer than males do.

They are also carnivores, meaning they only eat meat.

In Canada you can find Steller sea lions only on the West Coast.

Steller Sea Lion

If you ever see a sea lion sitting in the shape of a banana, don't worry! They sit this way to keep their back flippers and head warm.

Sea lions talk to each other with honks, grunts and other strange sounds.

What's a sea lion's favourite subject in school?

Art! Art! Art!

9

Belted kingfishers eat mostly small fish but will also eat crayfish, frogs, tadpoles and insects.

Female

Female belted kingfishers have a brown and a blue line across their chests. Males have only a blue line.

Male

Baby kingfishers can digest bones, shells and fish scales, but adult kingfishers cannot. This is because babies have more acid in their stomachs.

Kingfishers dig their own burrows and build their nests inside. The entrance to the burrow slopes upwards to keep water out of the nest.

Belted kingfishers live on the British Columbia coast all year round. Once breeding season starts, their range extends across Canada.

Where do fish sleep? On the river-bed!

Belted Kingfisher

11

Atlantic Puffin

Atlantic puffins can fly, but their wings are better used for swimming underwater where they catch their favourite food: fish!

They have spines in their mouth to keep the fish they catch from falling out.

Atlantic puffins are found only on the East Coast of Canada year round.

These birds shed their feathers once a year. While they are growing new ones, they can't fly.

Puffins build their nests in burrows they dig with their beak and the sharp claws on their toes.

Baby puffins are called pufflings.

13

North American river otters have thick fur that keeps them warm in cold water.

Their long whiskers are sensitive and help them find their way in dark or murky water.

To keep water out of their nose, river otters close their nostrils when they are underwater for a long time.

River otters often play together. They slide down the riverbank, chase their tails and play in the water.

These otters can be found throughout Canada in areas close to a water source such as rivers, lakes, ponds and marshes.

River otters are sensitive to dirty water. Their presence is a sign that the water is clean.

Where do otters keep their money?

In a riverbank!

North American River Otter

Yellow-bellied marmots are diurnal, meaning they are awake during the day and sleep at night

Yellow-bellied Marmot

Wuchak is the Cree word for marmot.

These creatures hibernate for 4 to 9 months of the year.

Marmot

Marmots are part of the squirrel family.

Marmots talk to each other with high pitched whistles and screams.

They live in parts of Alberta and British Columbia.

Hoary Marmot

What did the marmot say when he got his tail caught in the door?

It won't be long now!

Wolverines are brave, aggressive predators. They have sharp teeth and claws.

They have big, fluffy feet that act as snowshoes to help them stay on top of deep snow.

Wolverines save the food they don't eat by burying it and spraying it with musk. Musk has a strong scent that is disgusting to other animals.

Wolverine

Wolverines are more common in western Canada but can be found in northern Ontario, Manitoba and the territories.

Baby wolverines, called kits, stay with their mother for up to 2 years.

Wolverines are opportunistic hunters. This means they usually go after food that is close by and easy to catch. They will sometimes steal food from bears!

What's a wolverine's favourite arcade game?

The claw machine!

American coots bob their head back and forth when they walk and swim. Even coot chicks, which can walk and swim almost right after they are born, do it.

Coots run across the water to build up speed before they take off.

American coots live in southwestern British Columbia all year but spread across Canada when they are breeding.

American Coot

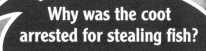

Why was the coot arrested for stealing fish?

Because he was coot in the act!

American coots eat mostly plants, but they will also eat insects and small creatures like tadpoles.

American coots don't have webbed feet. They have strange lobed feet with roundish flat pieces of skin on either side of their toes.

Their feet help the birds kick through the water and walk on soft mud.

21

The American bison is the largest land mammal in North America. There are two types, the wood bison and the slightly smaller plains bison. Male bison can weigh about 900 kg. That's heavier than a Volkswagen Beetle!

These animals are herbivores, meaning they eat plants. They can travel long distances to places that have more food.

Bison travel together in big groups called herds.

What do bison fathers say when their sons move away?

Bye-son!

Both female and male bison have horns, but the male's horns are much bigger than the female's.

In Lakota Sioux and other Indigenous tribes, the bison is sacred and is a comforting sign that food will be plentiful.

Few animals eat bison because of their large size. Wolves, bears and humans are their main predators.

Bison are found in parts of the Norhwest Territories, Yukon, British Columbia and the Prairies.

Sometimes a rare white bison is born. This happens only once in about 10 million births!

American Bison

Bighorn Sheep

Bighorn sheep have great balance and can climb steep rocky ledges to escape predators.

Male bighorn sheep are called rams, and females are called ewes.

Ewes usually stay with their mother's herd for the rest of their life. Rams and ewes travel in separate herds until breeding season.

The horns of a male bighorn sheep can weigh as much as all the rest of the bones in his body!

What do bighorn sheep wear to the beach?

A Baaaakini!

Bighorn sheep live in the Rocky Mountains and British Columbia's Coast Mountains.

To fight for access to females, rams bash heads by running towards each other at speeds of 64 kilometres per hour! That's faster than a car drives in the city!

Pronghorns can reach speeds of 96 kilometres per hour. That is as fast as a car driving on the highway!

They are the second fastest animal in the world!

Pronghorns use their white rump to communicate. When they see a predator, they lift the white hairs so the patch looks bigger and warns the rest of the herd.

How do pronghorns decorate for Christmas?

With horn-aments!

Pronghorn

In Canada, pronghorns can be found only in southern Alberta and Saskatchewan.

Pronghorns are ungulates. This means that they have hooves.

These mammals digest their food twice to make sure they absorb as many nutrients as possible.

Porcupine

They spend a lot of time alone. When they feel threatened by another porcupine, they chatter their teeth as a warning.

Porcupines don't move fast on land. They are often seen sitting in trees, munching on bark.

Porcupines can be found across Canada.

What is a porcupine's favourite game?

Poker!

A porcupine's teeth grow continuously, so it chews on bones, bark, leather and sticks to keep its teeth from getting too long.

Porcupines have about 30,000 quills! The quills have barbs, like fish hooks, which make them hard to take out if they get into your skin.

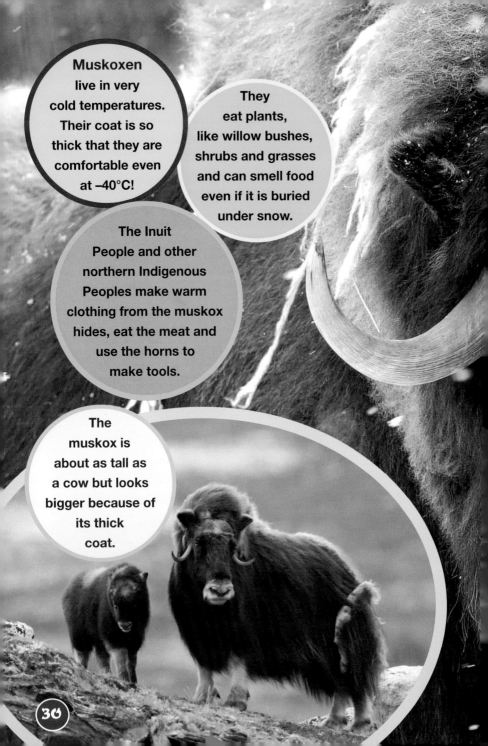

Muskoxen live in very cold temperatures. Their coat is so thick that they are comfortable even at −40°C!

They eat plants, like willow bushes, shrubs and grasses and can smell food even if it is buried under snow.

The Inuit People and other northern Indigenous Peoples make warm clothing from the muskox hides, eat the meat and use the horns to make tools.

The muskox is about as tall as a cow but looks bigger because of its thick coat.

Muskoxen

Muskoxen live in Nunavut and some parts of the Northwest Territories.

What do you call a muskox that has been sitting in storage?

A dust-ox!

The Kermode bear is a rare black bear born with white fur. They are also known as spirit bears for their ghostly fur colour.

Kermode bears hibernate in dens in the winter. They dig their own den or use hollowed out trees. Bear cubs are born in their dens during the winter.

Tsimshian coastal Indigenous Peoples call them moksgm'ol, meaning white bear.

Kermode Bear

Kermode bears are omnivores, meaning they eat both meat and plants. Male bears eat more salmon than females do.

The Kermode bear is the provincial animal of British Columbia!

These bears have a small range in northwestern British Columbia.

What do you call a bear with no teeth?

A gummy bear!

Painted turtles are cold-blooded, meaning that their body temperature is the same as the air temperature. They have to warm themselves in the sun by sitting on a rock or a log. Imagine doing that every time you get cold!

Western painted turtles can live to be more than 50 years old!

These turtles have a natural antifreeze in their bodies. They can survive temperatures as low as −9°C!

Western painted turtles can be found from southern British Columbia to Lake Superior in Ontario. They prefer warmer temperatures because of their cold blood.

The temperature of the turtle's nest affects the sex of the eggs in the nest! Warmer temperatures mean more female babies and colder temperatures mean more males.

What do you call a famous turtle?
A shell-ebrity!

Western Painted Turtle

Massasauga Rattlesnake

The Massasauga rattlesnake is venomous. It has a poisonous bite that it uses to kill its prey.

This snake only bites if it feels threatened.

It can be found in a small part of southern Ontario.

The rattlesnake's rattle is made of loose pieces of keratin. This is the same protein your fingernails are made from!

Massasauga rattlesnakes blend into their environment, helping them hide from both predators and prey!

Snakes eat mice and other small creatures. Snakes don't chew their food. They swallow it whole!

What is a snake's favourite school subject?

Hissstory!

37

Wood frogs eat insects, spiders and worms.

They are found in every province and territory in Canada.

Have you ever been on a walk and suddenly heard lots of frogs croaking or chirping? They are likely talking about you! Frogs use their voices to warn other frogs of predators and to talk to each other.

What do stylish frogs wear?

Jumpsuits!

They lay their eggs anywhere there is water. You can find pockets of eggs in small puddles, swamps and even water-filled ruts on gravel roads.

Most creatures would die if their bodies froze, but wood frogs have a natural anti-freeze in their blood. They can freeze in winter and then thaw in summer!

Frogs breathe through their skin, so they need clean water to survive. Many frogs in a pond or other body of water is always a good sign!

Wood Frog

Moose

Moose are good swimmers and can hold their breath for more than 30 seconds.

Moose live across Canada in forested areas near streams, ponds, lakes or marshes.

Moose are herbivores, meaning they eat only plants. Male moose are called bulls, and females are called cows.

The word moose means "eater of twigs" in the Algonquin language.

What is a moose's favourite sauce?

Moose-tard!

After mating season is over, bull moose shed their antlers. The antlers don't grow back until the next spring!

The flap of skin that hangs from the neck of a moose is called the dewlap.

Spotted skunks spray a musk when they feel threatened. They can spray this musk up to 4.5 metres, about the length of a minivan!

As a warning, they do a handstand before spraying.

It is a myth that tomato juice gets rid of skunk smell if you are unlucky enough to be sprayed! Instead, try washing with soap and baking soda.

Spotted skunks are found only in small parts of southern British Columbia, Manitoba and Ontario.

These skunks are nocturnal, meaning that they are active at night and sleep during the day.

Baby skunks are called kits.

Why did Jane bring her pet skunk to school?

For show and smell!

Spotted Skunk

Racoons, like humans, have opposable thumbs. This gives them better grip when climbing.

Their opposable thumbs also let them open things like containers, windows, locks on gates...pretty much anything they want to get in to!

The black mask and rings on its tail makes it look like a mischievous thief!

Raccoons are omnivores. They eat insects, bird eggs, fish, turtles, small mammals, berries, nuts and corn.

Racoon

Raccoons are known for raiding garbage cans and stealing fruit and vegetables from people's gardens.

Raccoons live throughout southern Canada.

What type of car does a raccoon drive?

A furr-ari!

Canada Goose

Canada geese can be found on the West Coast all year round but are spread throughout Canada during the breeding season.

Geese have spines on their tongue and beak called tomia. These spines help them hold onto slippery grass and other plants they pull from the ground to eat.

What side of the goose has the most feathers?

The outside!

Canada geese work together when they fly by forming a V in the sky. The goose in the front works the hardest, while the rest get a break. They switch positions often, so no one goose has to do all the work.

Geese that live on the western side of Canada tend to be darker in colour, while geese in eastern Canada tend to be lighter coloured.

47

The American pika lives in the Rocky Mountains in boulder fields, areas where boulders have piled up above the treeline.

American pikas collect grass in the summer and lay it on rocks in the sun to dry into hay. They pile the hay into haystacks in their dens so they will have food all winter.

They also steal hay from other pikas that live nearby.

American Pika

Pikas live alone and scare away other pikas that try to live too close.

What did the pika say when he saw his neighbour stealing his food?

Hay, come back!

Pikas talk to each other using high-pitched meeeeeeeep noises.

Great blue herons have hollow bones. Even though they are large birds, they weigh less than a large (4 litre) jug of milk!

They are found across southern Canada during the breeding season. They live year round on the coast of British Columbia and the Maritimes.

Great Blue Heron

Great blue herons catch fish by spearing them with their beak.

The great blue heron can be seen in swamps, by lakes and rivers and on ocean beaches.

The great blue heron has a patch of special feathers, called **powder down**, on its chest. The heron crumbles the down into a powder that it spreads through its other feathers to waterproof and clean slime and dirt off them.

How do great blue herons catch their dinner?

By spear fishing!

Muskrat

Muskrats can be found throughout all of Canada except for the Arctic Circle.

Muskrats have special teeth that allow them to chew underwater without opening their mouths.

What do muskrats eat for dessert?

Mice-cream!

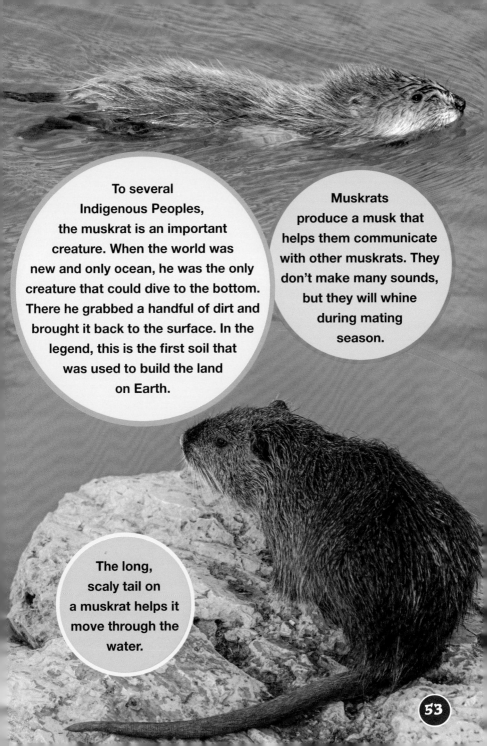

To several Indigenous Peoples, the muskrat is an important creature. When the world was new and only ocean, he was the only creature that could dive to the bottom. There he grabbed a handful of dirt and brought it back to the surface. In the legend, this is the first soil that was used to build the land on Earth.

Muskrats produce a musk that helps them communicate with other muskrats. They don't make many sounds, but they will whine during mating season.

The long, scaly tail on a muskrat helps it move through the water.

Wild Boar

Wild boars are fast runners and good swimmers!

The wild boar is an invasive species in some provinces. This means it is not a natural part of the ecosystem and affects the survival of other native species.

Why did it take the pig so long to catch up with his friends?

Because he was a slow-pork!

Wild boars are also known as wild pigs. They are nocturnal.

Most wild boars can be found in parts of southern Alberta and Saskatchewan with smaller populations in Quebec, Ontario and BC.

Wild boars use their sharp tusks to root (dig) for food. They use their nose to move dirt like a shovel.

They also use their tusks for self-defence.

Pileated woodpeckers hammer holes in trees to find food. Once they have made a hole in a tree trunk, they use their long tongue to catch bugs in the wood.

Woodpeckers hold onto trees with their sharp talons.

These woodpeckers hammer at trees with their strong, pointy beak. If you have ever heard a fast, loud knocking sound in the woods, it was probably a woodpecker!

Pileated Woodpecker

A pair of pileated woodpeckers will stay together all season!

What helps woodpeckers stick to the side of a tree?

Vel-crow!

These birds can be found in woodlands across Canada.

Why do foxes hunt rabbits?

Because they like fast food!

Swift foxes eat mostly rabbits and mice but will sometimes eat fruit when it's hard to find prey!

Swift foxes have a very small Canadian range in southern Alberta and Saskatchewan.

Swift foxes have good hearing and can even hear rodents digging underground!

These foxes keep their den all year round. They use it for shelter from predators, but also from the weather.

They can run as fast as a car drives in the city.

Swift Fox

Grey Wolf

Grey wolves are found throughout Canada except for some small sections of southern British Columbia, Alberta and Saskatchewan.

Adult wolves can eat up to 10 kilograms of meat in one meal. That's more than 80 hamburgers! But they don't eat everyday.

Grey wolves are also called timber wolves.

Wolves live in groups called packs. There is always a clear leader of the pack, called the alpha male.

Wolves howl to warn wolves that are not part of the pack away from their territory or to communicate with pack members who are far away.

What do you call a wolf that uses bad language?

A swearwolf!

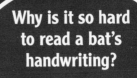

Why is it so hard to read a bat's handwriting?

Because it's usually upside down!

Little brown bats can be found across Canada.

Little brown bats are affected by a disease called white nose syndrome. This fungus kills almost all bats that are infected.

Never touch a dead bat with your bare hands. White nose syndrome does not affect humans, but you could accidentally spread it to other bats.

Little Brown Bat

Little brown bats are gregarious, meaning they live in large groups.

They use echolocation to find prey in the dark. Soundwaves from the calls the bats make bounce off nearby objects and echo back to the bat. From the echo, the bat can tell how big and how far away things are. The sounds bats make are so high pitched that human ears can't hear them.

Bats can eat about 1000 insects per night!

Snowshoe Hare

Snowshoe hares live across Canada except for parts of the Arctic Circle.

Snowshoe hares change colours with the seasons. They are white in the winter and brown in the summer. The colour change helps them blend in with their environment and hide from predators.

Snowshoe hares usually don't make any noise but will grunt at other hares to show that they are annoyed.

The snowshoe hare's feet prevent it from sinking into deep snow.

Where would snowshoe hares learn how to fly? In the hare-force!

In Mi'kmaq folklore, the rabbit got his long ears when it was lifted up by them. He told a lie that the sun would never rise again. When the other creatures found out that he had lied, the leader of the group lifted him out of the bushes by his ears, which stretched them to the length they are now.

65

Bobcats are nocturnal and rarely seen by humans.

They can be found across southern Canada.

Bobcats hunt by ambushing or sneaking up on their prey and pouncing on it.

Some big cats have long tails to help them balance on tall tree branches. Bobcats hunt on the ground, so they don't need a long tail to balance.

Bobcats usually eat small animals, like rabbits and mice, but will go much larger animals if they can.

What is a bobcat's favourite meal?

Mice Crispies!

Bobcat

Harp seals have claws on their front and back flippers. The strong claws on their front flippers help the seals pull themselves across the ice. The smaller back claws are used for grooming.

Indigenous Peoples use seal skin for gloves. The fur is thick and doesn't absorb much water.

Harp seals are found along the coast in Nunavut, Quebec, Labrador and Newfoundland.

Where do seals go to see the movies?

The dive-in!

Harp Seal

These adorable seals are white only when they are pups.

Harp seals stay warm with a type of fat called blubber. Pups develop a layer of blubber very quickly.

Harp seals can hold their breath underwater for 15 minutes!

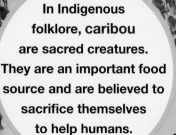

In Indigenous folklore, caribou are sacred creatures. They are an important food source and are believed to sacrifice themselves to help humans.

Wolves, grizzly bears and golden eagles are all predators of caribou. Golden eagles only go after newborn calves.

The fur on the antlers of caribou is called velvet. They shed their velvet during breeding season.

Caribou live throughout the Northwest Territories and northern regions of Alberta, Saskatchewan, Manitoba, Ontario, Quebec and Labrador.

Caribou

Caribou are always travelling and following signs that there is food nearby. They travel in large groups called herds.

Caribou have large hooves that keep them from sinking into snow and the mossy, soft ground in the deep tundra.

Domestic caribou are also known as reindeer.

What did the caribou say to his wife when he looked at the sky?

I think it's going to rain, dear!

Pine Marten

Pine martens are great climbers! Their long claws and thick fur on the bottom of their paws helps them grip the tree as they climb.

Pine martens live throughout Canada but avoid the southern regions of Manitoba and Saskatchewan.

Pine martens are agile creatures and can easily escape many predators.

How did the pine marten send a message across the forest?

With moss code!

Pine martens eat birds, fruit, nuts and even snowshoe hares!

They use tree hollows or the holes made by pileated woodpeckers as dens.

Baby martens, called kits, live in their den until they are fully grown.

Snowy Owl

Snowy owls' white feathers help them blend in with the snow.

What do snowy owls use after every bath?

A t-owl!

Male snowy owls have more white feathers than females. Harry Potter's Hedwig was actually a male owl!

Snowy owls live in the northern regions of Nunavut and the Northwest Territories during the breeding season. Some st in the Arctic year round, and others fly south in winter to the provinces east of British Columbia.

When snowy owls fly, they stay close to the ground to watch for food. They eat mice and other small rodents.

To many Indigenous Peoples, owls are said to carry messages from the Spirit World.

These owls have thick, heavy feathers for insulation from the cold arctic weather. Even their feet are feathery!

75

Most of the time, the eagle cry you hear in movies is the call of a red-tailed hawk.

Red-tailed hawks are found throughout Canada.

During breeding season, the male shows off by grabbing the female in midair! They hold onto each other and freefall for a few moments, then fly gracefully away.

Red-tailed Hawk

Red-tailed hawks are a common sight. They are often seen circling in the air or perched on a something tall to search for food. They have sharp, powerful talons.

These large hawks only weigh about as much as an average-sized laptop because their bones are hollow.

What type of phone does a hawk use?

A hawkie talkie!

Masked Shrew

Masked shrews eat a lot of food for their size. They will sometimes eat up to 3 times their weight in food!

What sound do shrews make when they sneeze?

A-Shrew!

These shrews have a strong odour that keeps many predators away, but hawks, snakes and even large frogs eat them.

Masked shrews live throughout Canada.

The masked shrew is about the same size as a mouse. You can easily tell a shrew from a mouse by the shrew's pointed snout.

Shrews are nocturnal, meaning they are active at night.

The Publisher: iThink Books

iThink Books is an imprint of Folklore Publishing Ltd.
www.folklorepublishing.com

Library and Archives Canada Cataloguing in Publication

Title: Laugh out loud: Canadian nature / Sahara Kagume.

Other titles: Canadian nature

Names: Kagume, Sahara, author.

Identifiers: Canadiana (print) 20220187231 | Canadiana (ebook) 2022018724X | ISBN

9781897206331 (softcover) | ISBN 9781897206386 (PDF)

Subjects: LCSH: Canada—Juvenile humor. | LCSH: Nature—Juvenile humor. | LCSH: Canada

—Miscellanea—Juvenile literature. | LCSH: Nature—Miscellanea—Juvenile literature. | LCSH:

Wit and humor, Juvenile. | CSH: Canadian wit and humor (English)—Juvenile literature. |

LCGFT: Humor.

Classification: LCC PN6231.C19 K34 2022 | DDC jC818/.602—dc23

Cover Image Credits:

Frontcover: GettyImages-frentusha; Andrii Shelenkov.

Backcover: GettyImages-Donyanedomam; SWKrulllmaging; Moose Henderson

Photo credits: Every effort has been made to accurately credit the sources of photographs and illustrations. Any errors or omissions should be reported directly to the publisher for correction in future editions. From Getty Images Credit- mtnmichelle, 73; passion4nature, 45; Weber, 63; Dan Rieck, 51; JMrocek, 55; Susan Perry, 75; abriggs21, 50; rubynurbaidi, 28, 29; MajaPhoto, 59; CreativeNature_nl, 79; slowmotiongli, 18, 66, 68, 69; Carol Hamilton, 51; AntiMartina,25; JMrocek, 55; jamesvancouver, 75; JMrocek, 54; RichardGalbraith, 11; gkuchera, 66; Layne vanRhijn, 58; bobloblaw, 53; Platinka, 13; pleshko74, 15; Lucie Kasparova, 17; Geoffrey Reynaud, 70; RichardSeeley, 70; siridhata pronghorn, 26; AB Photography, 61; Rohit Kumar, 9; IgorZakowski, 19; Devonyu, 56; Tigatelu, 6; MarcStephan, 52; serfeo, 53; eZeePics Studio, 62; Dennis Holcomb Photography, 76; Jim_Pintar, 74; Dreamcreation, 38; Tigatelu, 40, 3, 37; Mulyadi, 35; hermandesign2015, 31; Mimomy, 33; Myriam Pare, 31; NATALIIA OMELCHENKO, 2, 4; DanielLacy, 14; Frank Fichtmüller, 30; 6381380, 7; passion4nature, 21; Susan Perry,46; BrianEKushner, 7; MHaen, 47; BrianEKushner, 71; Steve Adams, 12; Janet Griffin-Scott, 46; bobloblaw, 26; Stu Weiss, 27; ca2hill, 39; JohnPitcher, 37; jcrader, 49, 5; Alan Levy, 6; Jason_Ray_Photography, 23; DaveGartland, 36; BrianLasenby, 49; moose, 48; Jillian Cooper, 22; Nicola_Romano,16; Shoemcfly, 36; Donyanedomam, 38; StarlightImages, 39; Brams-Photography, 13 ; Jeff Kingma, 20; seb29, 45; MEGiordano_Photography, 41; JenDeVos, 21; Veriditas Rising, 29; mlharing, 73, 72; Monica Lara, 67; ChrisGorgio, 65; janeff, 64; AB Photography, 60; impr2003, 65; mtnmichelle, 73; ArendTrent, 64; janeff, 64; Carol ,29; Shayne Kaye, 35; Shoemcfly, 36; Paul Hartley, 28; Scott Canning, 32; karlumbriaco, 44; Trek13, 35, tvirbickis, 34; Michel VIARD, 33; mirceax, 57; mlharing, 25; Yuqun, 25; twildlife, 26; BrianEKushner, 77; rancho_runner, 77; Weber lighter, 42; belizar73,19; Wildnerdpix, 17; LagunaticPhoto, 14; DanielLacy, 15; photographybyJHWilliams, 9 ; Tigatelu, 61; Myriam Pare, 4 BrianEKushner, 10; Weber, 5, 43; Dualororua, 51; Bullet_Chained, 47, 3; Nenilkime,72; pilipenkoD,8; Mimosa Studio, 71; lineartestpilot, 78; johnnylemonseed,62; Dmitry Zyrin, 52; Rynn_malkavian, 67; Sally Hinton, 15; sababaJJ, 57; ridjam, 77; SteveByland, 11; Lisa Lebedeva, 43; LeeDaniels, 68; Bborriss, 9; Mimosa Studio, 54; julos, 2; ayutaka, 58; Denja1, 18; Hemera Technologies,19; dmbaker, 22; RichardSeeley, 20; Ferenc Cegledi, 16; SWKrulllmaging,24

We acknowledge the financial support of the Government of Canada.
Nous reconnaissons l'appui financier du gouvernement du Canada.

Funded by the Government of Canada | Financé par le gouvernement du Canada | Canadä

Produced with the assistance of the Government of Alberta. Alberta

PC: 38-1

Printed in China